OZARKS

OZARKS

PHOTOGRAPHY BY DAVID FITZGERALD
TEXT BY CLAY ANDERSON

GRAPHIC ARTS CENTER PUBLISHING COMPANY
PORTLAND, OREGON

International Standard Book Number 0-912856-94-7
Library of Congress Catalog Card Number 85-71194
© MCMLXXXV by Graphic Arts Center Publishing Company
P.O. Box 10306, Portland, Oregon 97210 • 503/226-2402
Editor-in-Chief • Douglas A. Pfeiffer
Designer • Robert Reynolds
Typographer • Paul O. Giesey/Adcrafters
Printer • Rono Graphic Communications
Bindery • Lincoln and Allen
Printed in the United States of America
Second Printing

Frontispiece: Once prone to wild flooding, the White River is now controlled by dams for most of its first two hundred miles. It heads up in the Boston Mountains, near Fayetteville, Arkansas, flows west, then north into Missouri, turns east, and then south back into Arkansas. The river's course is a series of lakes beginning with Beaver Lake near the headwaters, then Table Rock, Taneycomo, and finally Bull Shoals, shown here near Spring Creek, Arkansas.

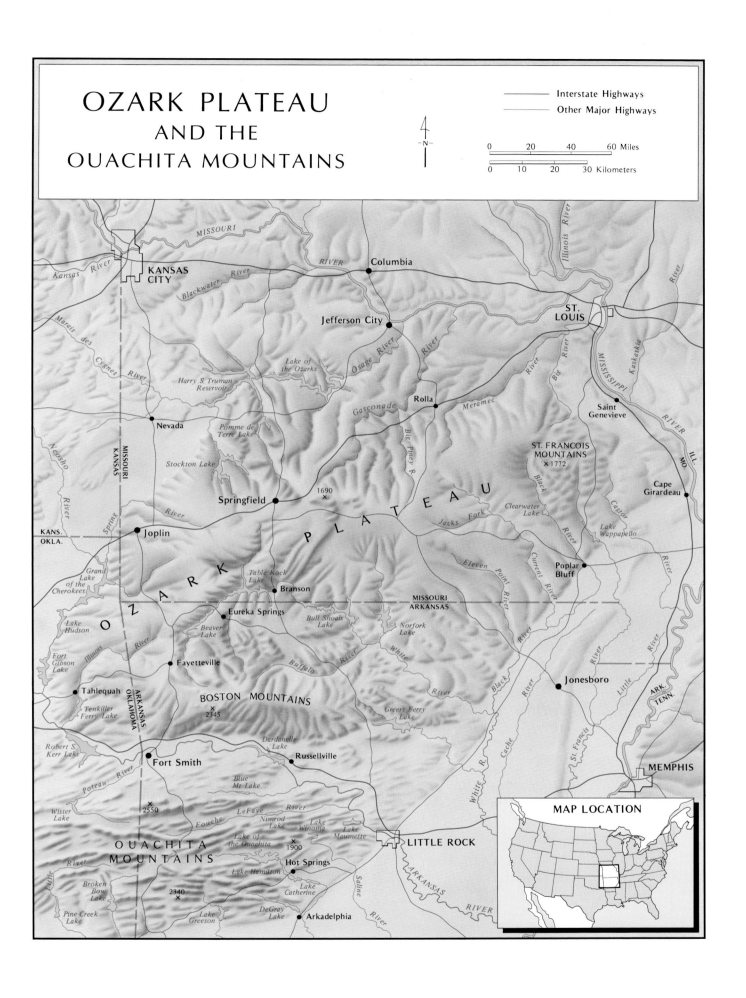

OZARK PLATEAU
AND THE
OUACHITA MOUNTAINS

Interstate Highways
Other Major Highways

0   20   40   60 Miles
0   10   20   30 Kilometers

-N-

MISSOURI

Kansas River

KANSAS CITY

Blackwater River

RIVER

Columbia

ST. LOUIS

Illinois River

Jefferson City

Marais des Cygnes River

Osage River

Lake of the Ozarks

Harry S. Truman Reservoir

Gasconade

Rolla

Big River

Kaskaskia

MISSOURI
KANSAS

Nevada

Pomme de Terre Lake

Meramec

Saint Genevieve

MISSISSIPPI

Stockton Lake

Big Piney R.

ST. FRANCOIS MOUNTAINS
×1772

Neosho River

1690 ×

Springfield

Black

Clearwater Lake

Cape Girardeau

MO.

ILL.

Spring River

River

Jacks Fork

Castor River

Lake Wappapello

KANS.
OKLA.

Joplin

Current River

Poplar Bluff

Grand Lake of the Cherokees

O Z A R K   P L A T E A U

Table Rock Lake

Eleven Point River

River

Lake Hudson

Branson

MISSOURI
ARKANSAS

Eureka Springs

Beaver Lake

Bull Shoals Lake

Norfork Lake

Fort Gibson Lake

Illinois River

Buffalo River

White

Black River

River

Little River

Fayetteville

Jonesboro

Tahlequah

BOSTON MOUNTAINS
×2345

Greers Ferry Lake

ARK.
TENN.

Tenkiller Ferry Lake

St. Francis River

Robert S. Kerr Lake

Dardanelle Lake

ARKANSAS
OKLAHOMA

Russellville

Cache River

MEMPHIS

Fort Smith

Blue Mt. Lake

Poteau River

×2550

Wister Lake

LeFave River

Nimrod Lake

Lake Winona

Lake Maumelle

White R.

Fouche

Lake of the Ouachita

×1900

LITTLE ROCK

OUACHITA MOUNTAINS

Lake Hamilton

Hot Springs

Arkansas River

Little River

×2340

Lake Catherine

Saline River

ARKANSAS

Broken Bow Lake

Lake Greeson

DeGray Lake

Arkadelphia

RIVER

Pine Creek Lake

MAP LOCATION

5

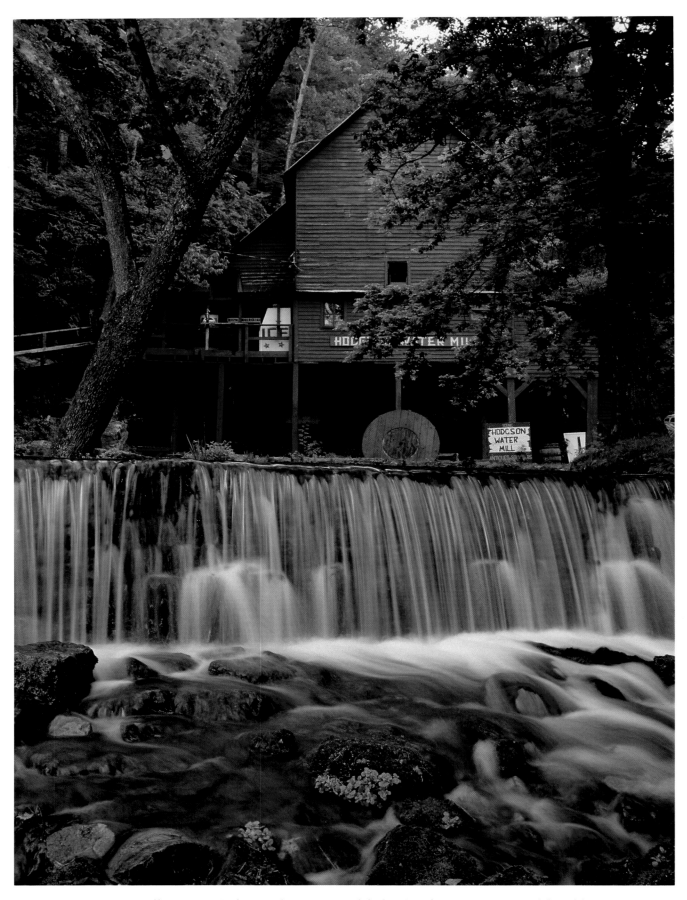

Grist mills were a vital part of community life for Ozark pioneers. Five of the old mills are still standing in Ozark County, Missouri, which was so isolated it was not reached by paved roads until the 1950s. A spring flowing 23 million gallons of water per day has powered Hodgson Mill since the Civil War, and the mill's trademark appears on stone-buhr-ground products sold around the nation.

INTRODUCTION

When I was living in the sprawling Chicago metropolitan area and pining to be in the Ozarks, one day I came across a very tiny newspaper advertisement buried in the paper. The small headline declared: "All the lies they tell about the Ozarks are true."

That statement was as much of an enigma as my own feelings. What was this longing within me? I grew up in the hills of Southeast Missouri. I visited relatives living at Bonne Terre in the "Lead Belt," my Uncle Roy Magill took me fishing on the St. Francis and Black rivers, and my mother's family gathered at places like Big Spring, Lake Killarney, Mine La Motte, and Castor River for picnics and outings. I remember filling an enamel cup at Big Spring with my Aunt Mary Dale holding on to my shirttail when I was only two years old. Lakes were few and far between in the Ozarks when I was a boy, and Lake Killarney was an aqueous jewel set miraculously in the St. Francois Mountains. When I went back in later years, Lake Killarney was something of a disappointment, but Big Spring is magnificent to this day.

A cold river appearing to boil out of the base of a rugged hill, Big Spring is estimated to have had a maximum flow of 840 million gallons a day, the largest flow in the United States and one of the largest in the world. Big Spring actually emerges from the wreckage of a cave outlet and, on an average day, discharges 276 million gallons, which is tops in a region particularly noted for its springs.

But life in the Ozarks was typified more by small springs, the kind of springs people sheltered with spring houses and used as natural refrigeration for milk, cream, butter, eggs, and fresh produce. That represented a way of life, and for me the personification of the Ozarks was Uncle Bill Anderson.

Uncle Bill was a route mail carrier in Kansas City in the 1930s when he began to yearn for the Ozarks. Possibly, some of his feelings were as vague as mine in later years, but there was nothing vague about his love of fishing. With his family and another couple there were many trips to the Osage River in the Warsaw, Missouri area, and sometime in the early 1930s, about the time Lake of the Ozarks began filling, Uncle Bill decided where he wanted to be.

He advertised in a postal paper his willingness to trade his city route for one in the Ozarks, received a favorable response, and moved his family into a house near Brumley, Missouri. The family farmed and gardened, kept livestock, and worked hand in hand with their neighbors. And of course, Uncle Bill carried the mail, always over rough country roads, punishing to

vehicles, and when he could not cover the route otherwise he would resort to horseback.

Even with farming and carrying the mail, Uncle Bill always found time for fishing. Lake of the Ozarks was relatively new, and the fishing was great. Bagnell Dam, built by Union Electric Company, had impounded some sixty-five-thousand acres of water surface with thirteen hundred miles of shoreline. It was the second of the large man-made lakes in the Ozarks, but it was far larger than its predecessor, Lake Taneycomo, created in 1913 by Powersite Dam, which was built on the White River near Forsyth, Missouri.

After Uncle Bill retired, he and Aunt Zella moved to California. I visited them there while on a business trip, and the hearty laugh that seemed to come from the depths of his short, powerful body was still the same. He was holding down two jobs and fishing in the ocean. He was still the same, but it didn't seem quite right to me.

Some time after I moved back to the Ozarks, Uncle Bill and Aunt Zella did too. They built a new house on a small acreage north of Brumley and began gardening as if they were trying to forestall a world famine. Uncle Bill's catch of fish would have prevented a lot of hunger, too. Often I dropped by their place at mealtime and feasted on fresh fried fish, parboiled raccoon baked with dressing, fresh asparagus and six or eight other homegrown vegetables, strawberries, and two kinds of pie at one sitting.

There is not much to see in Brumley any more, a striking contrast to the nearby Lake of the Ozarks tourist area. At one time, there were three stores, and Uncle Bill and Aunt Zella operated one. Now only one store remains, and the children are bused to a consolidated school. But there is a strong community spirit. Uncle Bill and some of his friends founded a Lions Club, a surprising idea for what at first glance appears to be just a shell of a little Ozarks town. The club is small, but active and enthusiastic, and has built a community center. It was in the basement of this building that we shared a special Thanksgiving dinner.

I envisioned a family affair, and it was, but Uncle Bill's family had grown. It was attended by four generations of kin, along with children they helped raise, neighbors they had helped and who had helped them, people they worked with in church, the pastor and former pastors, fishing buddies, fellow gardeners, Lions Club members, mail route patrons, farmers Uncle Bill had traded work with, housewives with whom Aunt Zella had shared kitchen tasks — maybe one hundred and fifty people. Maybe more. And not one stranger.

I have observed this Ozarks miracle of generosity and hard work many times. From the last day of school basket dinners at the old Fruitland School through family reunions, church suppers, baptisms, all day singings, and funerals — a multitude assembles and a few unsung, self-effacing ladies produce a feast.

But at this Thanksgiving dinner, I thought they had overshot their mark. My first time through the line, I took small portions, so sure was I that there would not be enough to feed this crowd. But more food appeared, and I filled my plate twice more, and then tasted all the different pies and cakes.

In April of the following year, Uncle Bill died. One does not expect to see a traffic jam in Brumley, but there was one on the day of Uncle Bill's funeral. Every seat in the Christian Church was filled, and we stood with many others along the walls. The service was personal. Uncle Bill knew his minister, and his minister knew Uncle Bill. The minister cited Uncle Bill's favorite Bible verse from The General Epistle of James:

Even so faith, if it hath not works, is dead, being alone. (2:17)

GEOGRAPHY: A DEFINED VAGUENESS

The geology, history, folklore, and culture of the Ozarks are distinct, but the precise thing that makes the Ozarks unique remains nebulous. Most likely, it has to do with the people, who shape the land and are shaped by it.

Most people are as vague about what and where the Ozarks are as they are about its name. There are a number of theories, but the most plausible is that the name evolved from the French, *aux arcs. Aux* is a preposition meaning *of, to,* or *from,* while *arcs* signifies *hills* or *bows.* The pronunciation of *aux arcs* is roughly the same as *Ozarks.*

Distinct in some places, the boundaries of the region are virtually indistinguishable in others. Just south of Cape Girardeau, Missouri, the hills end precisely where the delta country begins. This abrupt geological division continues southwestward, eventually meeting and following the Black River. At places such as Poplar Bluff, Missouri, and Black Rock, Arkansas, one drives through rolling hills, crosses a bridge, and emerges in flatlands. Downstream from the place where the Black River joins White River, the Ozarks boundary arcs to the west. Meeting and following the Arkansas River Valley upstream into Oklahoma, the boundary then swings north along the Neosho River, close to the point at which it joins the Arkansas. The Ozarks border then proceeds northeastward, catching just the southeast

corner of Kansas and continuing to Boonville, Missouri, on the Missouri River. Then it turns east, approximately following the Missouri to Pacific, Missouri, near St. Louis, where it cuts across and follows the Mississippi to Cape Girardeau. Some authorities say the region includes two Illinois counties across the river and north of Cape Girardeau, and the residents of this area have lately taken some pride in promoting the "Southern Illinois Ozarks."

In his book *The Ozarks: Land and Life,* Dr. Milton D. Rafferty, head of the Department of Geography and Geology at Southwest Missouri State University in Springfield, calls the Ozarks a parallelogram, including parts of four states, but not including the Southern Illinois hills. Rafferty points out that the Ozarks form part of a larger province called the Interior Highlands, which extends the parallelogram some one hundred miles to the southeast, taking in the Arkansas Valley and the Ouachita Mountains. Dr. Rafferty also notes that the region is variously called the Ozark Mountains, Ozark Plateau or Plateaus, Ozark Upland, Ozark Highland and Ozark Hill Country. He prefers upland because it has "a very general meaning." I prefer "The Ozarks" because it is less specific and more magical.

Mountaineers is an apt enough description for the people, but in truth the Ozarks are not very mountainous. The St. Francois Mountains in Eastern Missouri and the Bostons and Ouachitas in Arkansas come closest to qualifying as mountains. The igneous rocks of the St. Francois Mountains are not found elsewhere in the Ozarks or Ouachitas. As the overlying sedimentary rocks weather and erode, the once molten rocks are slowly exposed, along with knobs of granite and felsite. Where streams force through these resistant rocks, there are rugged gorges called "shut-ins." In *Geologic Wonders and Curiosities of Missouri,* Thomas R. Beveridge wrote that, "Intensively fractured igneous rock is commonly exposed in our Ozark shut-ins. This fracturing has contributed to the beauty, helping to produce vertical canyon walls and pinnacles as well as a maze of stream patterns with potholes and water-polished, naturally sculpted igneous rocks."

Johnson Shut-ins, fourteen miles southwest of Ironton, Missouri, the best known though not the largest, has seen development as a state park, as has Millstream Gardens. Stouts Creek Shut-ins, just above Lake Killarney, shares Johnson and Millstream's easy accessibility. Thirty-seven other accessible and popular shut-ins located in St. Francois, Iron, Wayne, Madison, Washington, and Reynolds counties are listed in Beveridge's book.

The Ozarks and Ouachitas are dotted with large and small lakes, virtually all man-made in this century. Lake Fort Smith has only nine hundred surface acres, but it is particularly scenic from U.S. 71 near Mountainburg, Arkansas. A 125-acre state park is located just below the dam. Lake Fort Smith, along with nearby Lake Shepherd Springs, provides water to the city of Fort Smith.

A fisherman enjoys the peaceful solitude of Table Rock Lake while casting from a favorite point. The nearby dam forming this large lake was built in 1958. The lake contains warm-water fish including bass, channel catfish and crappie.

The highest point in Missouri, Taum Sauk Mountain, has an elevation of 1,772 feet above sea level and is part of the St. Francois Mountains. Nearby is cone-shaped Pilot Knob. The Taum Sauk Trail leads hikers to Mina Sauk Falls, which cascades 132 feet; to Devils Toll Gate, an eight foot-wide, thirty foot-high and fifty foot-long opening in reddish igneous rock; to Johnson Shut-Ins; and to Elephant Rocks, a stationary herd of pink boulders near Graniteville.

While the St. Francois Mountains hold many geological wonders and curiosities, the Boston Mountains are higher, stand out in greater relief, and are truer to Ozark landscape. Elevations of more than two thousand feet are found over much of Madison, Washington, Franklin, Johnson, Pope, and Newton counties in Arkansas. The Boston Mountains are a relatively smooth, though far from flat, plateau surface. South of Jasper, Highway 7 follows a high ridge overlooking the broad Limestone Valley, which lies more than one thousand feet below. The Richwoods basin in Stone County is a similar pocket of agricultural prosperity, and there are lesser basins throughout the Bostons. South of Fayetteville, U.S. 71 follows a high, broad ridge affording a vista of broad valleys.

Cutting through the Boston Mountains is the Buffalo River, flowing to its confluence with the White River which skirts the Bostons to the northeast. Many of the more spectacular geological formations of the Bostons lie in the watershed of the Buffalo: Lost Valley, Big Bluff, Hemmed-in-Hollow, and many caves, natural bridges, waterfalls, and spectacular bluffs.

In addition to the St. Francois and Boston mountains, Dr. Rafferty lists seven other geographic regions within the Ozarks: the White River Hills along the Arkansas-Missouri border; the Springfield Plain, mostly west and south of Springfield, Missouri; the Central Plateau, a large slice running east to west through the middle of the region; the Osage-Gasconade Hills, including a large portion of the watersheds of those two rivers and Lake of the Ozarks; the Courtois Hills, west and south of the St. Francois Mountains, including the watersheds of the Current and Eleven Point rivers; the Missouri River Border; and the Mississippi River Border.

If that is not complicated enough, there are areas identified in the vernacular. "The Cookson Hills" and "Cherokee Country" of Northeast Oklahoma and the "Tri-State District" around Joplin, Missouri, are all on the Springfield Plain. "Shepherd of the Hills Country" and "White River Country" are included in the White River Hills. Both the "Boonslick Region" and "Missouri Rhineland" lie in the Missouri River Border. The "River Hills Region" falls within the Mississippi River Border. The "Tiff Belt," the "Lead Belt" and the "New Lead Belt" identify parts of the St. Francois Mountains. "The Irish Wilderness" is found in the steep and wild terrain of the Courtois Hills.

So that is the Ozarks, some sixty thousand square miles in all. Through my layman's eyes, only the St. Francois Mountains and parts of the Springfield Plain are quickly distinguishable. But whether the terrain is gently rolling or steep and rugged, it presents an endless variety of springs, caves, sinkholes, bluffs, glades, forests of oak and other hardwoods, cedars and pines, clear-flowing streams and, through the intervention of man, large lakes.

The Ozarks are not particularly high in elevation. An understanding of the land is aided by the word "plateau." Picking out the higher points in all directions, one can imagine these points were once all part of a fairly level plateau. Countless rains and snows fell, gradually cutting away portions of the soil and the underlying sedimentary rocks, which are limestone, dolomite, and chert. The waters, which penetrated the surface through faults and fissures, carved underground streams and, aided by naturally formed acids, caves of all sizes.

Over the eons, the erosion—both above and below the surface—changed the plateau into a region of hills and valleys of widely varying size, with networks of brooks, creeks, and rivers flowing off to the north, east, and south into the Missouri, Mississippi, and Arkansas rivers. Today, these hills and hollows are heavily forested. Oak is the predominant hardwood, accompanied by hickory, ash, elm, black walnut, and a number of other species. Either cedar or pine—both seldom thrive in the same locale at the same time—are intermingled in the woodlands.

The Ozarks Plateau and the adjoining Arkansas Valley and Ouachita Mountains—or the Interior Highlands as the combined region is called—are almost surrounded by plains. To the west are the Osage Plains of Missouri, Kansas, Oklahoma, and Texas; to the north, the Till Plains of Missouri and Illinois; to the east, the Mississippi Alluvial Plain of Southeast Missouri and Eastern Arkansas, and to the south, the West Gulf Coastal Plain of Southern Arkansas and Oklahoma. Only by that little range of hills called the Illinois Ozarks do the Ozarks link up with other uplands. In fact, those hills of extreme Southern Illinois—sometimes called the Shawneetown Hills—may just as properly be considered part of the low limestone plateau to their east in Kentucky, Tennessee, and Indiana.

EARLY SETTLERS

The ties with the hills of Kentucky and Tennessee and with the Appalachians further east are more than purely geographical. Many of the earliest settlers of the Ozarks came from Eastern Kentucky and Tennessee, Virginia and North Carolina. The earliest white Ozark settlements were begun in earnest along the Mississippi and Missouri rivers one hundred years before settlements in the interior hinterlands. Marquette and Joliet had explored the Mississippi, and in 1682 La Salle claimed the Mississippi Valley (and the Ozarks) for France. The French ceded the Province of Louisiana to Spain in 1762, took it back in 1800, and sold it to the United States in 1803.

The salt, lead, and fur trades attracted the French. The earliest French settlements spread from Kaskaskia, which was established in 1699 on the Illinois side of the Mississippi, across from Ste. Genevieve which was established in 1735. Interest in the salt springs to the south and the lead ore in the St. Francois Mountains to the west spurred these settlements, as well as Mine La Motte, established in 1723, Bonne Terre, established in 1724, and Old Mines, established in 1725. The French also established Fort Orleans on the Missouri, just outside of the Ozarks, in 1722. Down the Mississippi, Cape Girardeau was begun in 1793 during the Spanish period, as was Jackson, in 1799, and Potosi, in 1798.

The French, and later the Spanish, sent expeditions into the interior of the Ozarks seeking gold and silver. Inevitably, some mines were salted with silver and the legend of silver mines in the region's folklore continues to this day. The French also explored the southern reaches of the Ozarks: Marquette and Joliet reached the mouth of the Arkansas River in 1673; La Salle visited the village of the Quapaws in the vicinity of present day Little Rock in 1682; and one of La Salle's lieutenants, searching for his missing leader, founded Arkansas Post near the confluence of the White and Arkansas rivers in 1686.

By 1800, the American frontier had pushed to the extreme eastern edge of the Ozarks, but the main thrust of western migration went around the region. Batesville, Arkansas, on the White River at the southern edge of the Ozarks, was founded in 1812. Greenville, Missouri, fifty miles west of Cape Girardeau on the St. Francis River was founded in 1819, but Van Buren, twenty-five miles further west on the Current River, was not begun until 1859.

The Ozark interior was forbidding. Warsaw, Missouri, which lies on the Osage River near the western edge of the Ozarks, had its inception in 1826, but Springfield, Missouri, which was to become the Ozarks' largest city and its most important trading center, was not founded until 1830. Fort Smith, a military post at the confluence of the Arkansas and Poteau rivers, was established to protect travelers and to control Indians in 1817, but Fayetteville, fifty miles north, did not see its beginning until 1837.

There is evidence that several ancient civilizations lived in the Ozarks, but in 1800, when the white man's western migration was poised at the Mississippi, the Osage Indians dominated the vast, rugged territory stretching from the Missouri on the north to Arkansas on the south and west to the plains. Some of North America's most warlike Indians, they raided white settlements and fought on numerous occasions with other tribes.

Although Osage claims to most of the Ozarks were relinquished in a treaty in 1808, the tribe contended it had given up only land, not hunting rights. Its forays led it into conflict with the Kickapoos, Cherokees, Piankashaws, Shawnees, Weas, Peorias, and Delawares, who had given up lands east of the Mississippi for former Osage lands.

The Osages had developed a hunting-gathering-farming economy whose emphasis was hunting. Their system was well suited to the Ozarks, and it is interesting to note that the settlers who supplanted them had a somewhat similar economy, with their emphasis on farming. That emphasis, plus the white man's tendency to overpopulate the fragile land, was to be his undoing.

Years after the establishment of settlements on the region's perimeter, the interior of the Ozarks remained dangerous. Henry Rowe Schoolcraft, who provided the first studious report on an unknown portion of the Louisiana Purchase, wrote in his *Journal of a Tour into the Interior of Missouri and Arkansas* in 1818 and 1819 that few approved his journey at the outset, and all united in considering it "very hazardous." Leaving Potosi with a companion and a packhorse, Schoolcraft followed the Osage Trace, explored the valleys of the Merrimack and Current rivers, may have been the first white man to set eyes on Mammoth Spring, visited settlements on Sugar Loaf Prairie and Beaver Creek, followed the Osage Trace up Swan Creek, crossed over to the James River, and descended the White by canoe before returning to Potosi. Schoolcraft visited with widely scattered settlers and hunters; encountered Indians, wolves, and buffalo; hunted deer, bear, turkey, and wild honey; ate acorns, pumpkin, boiled buffalo bones, and beaver tail; and made copious notes on the terrain, rocks, fauna, and flora.

Eureka Springs, Arkansas, sprang into being in 1879 after pioneer doctor Alvah Jackson attributed miraculous cures to the waters of Basin Spring. By the time the Rosalie House was built in 1883, Eureka Springs had five thousand residents and was the third largest city in Arkansas. The elegant Victorian-style home with its elaborate woodwork and handmade bricks has been restored and is open for tours.

Known in the Ozarks as the "Flaming Fall Revue," or the "Festival of the Painted Leaves," the coloring of hardwood trees in autumn is much anticipated and the subject of widespread speculation. Predicting how and when the leaves will turn color is risky, as oaks, hickories, and sycamores present a variety of hues. Yellows and orange predominate in this grove near Spavinaw, Oklahoma.

The geography and geology of the region are easily recognizable today from Schoolcraft's descriptions, but the hardships he endured can only be imagined. The buffalo, wolves, and panthers exist no longer, and turkey and bear survive only because of re-stocking programs. His descriptions of the forests remain accurate, save for the replacement of virgin hardwoods and pines with smaller specimens. He describes vaster grasslands than one can imagine and makes no mention of red cedars, which have spread widely through the Ozarks, thriving on abandoned homesteads.

Schoolcraft wrote, "I begin my tour where other travellers have ended theirs," but within ten years a wave of migration was filtering into the remote hills and hollows of the Ozarks. It was a special breed of people who chose the Ozarks when more promising lands lay to the north, west, and south. Those who came selected lands close to rivers, creeks, and springs for they had chosen a life that demanded self-sufficiency.

Russell Gerlach's *Immigrants in the Ozarks* reveals the pattern of settlement in the Missouri Ozarks. In 1830, only Missouri and Mississippi river border sections had population densities of two to six people per square mile. The southwestern quarter of the state was virtually uninhabited. The next push was along the western edge of the Ozarks into the Springfield Plain, leaving only a large bulge at the Arkansas line without significant population. By 1850, the empty area was beginning to disappear, and areas to the west, north, and east were showing considerable growth. In the census of 1860, all parts of the Ozarks showed some population, and Gerlach notes the "dominance of Tennessee stock over much of the rougher and less productive Ozarks, while Kentucky and Virginia stock dominated the more productive Ozark borders." Many of these Tennessee settlers were descendants of North Carolinians who followed a similar pattern in search of available lands.

The settling of the Ozarks continued throughout the nineteenth century. There were large German settlements in the Mississippi and Missouri borders and smaller pockets of Germans on the Springfield Plain. French, Swedish, Polish, Moravian, Austrian, Swiss, Dutch, and other ethnic groups settled in certain communities whose locations were determined by early railroad construction, particularly the Springfield-St. Louis route.

The settlement of the Ozarks was impeded by the Civil War. Although Missouri had been admitted to the Union as a slave state, there was little interest in slavery in a region where only a tiny fraction of the land made it economically attractive. Still, the Ozarks was divided on all the other issues attending the war, and the region was contested in two major battles, Wilson's Creek in Missouri and Pea Ridge in Arkansas, and in many lesser battles and skirmishes. A no-man's-land during the conflict, the Ozarks was preyed upon by bushwhackers, deserters, renegades, and guerrillas. Few buildings survived the war, and bitterness continued in its aftermath as vigilante groups sought to correct wrongs and impose law and order.

For the most part, the people of the Ozarks were more concerned with just getting by. They built their homes from logs hewed in the forests, heated them with wood burned in native-rock fireplaces, and raised livestock, gardens, corn, and sometimes cotton or tobacco as cash crops. They also gathered nuts and berries from the wilds and herbs for homemade medicines, hunted wild game for food, and trapped fur-bearers as another source of cash. They provided their own entertainment and followed the customs, traditions, and religion they had brought with them.

Taney County, Missouri, south of Springfield on the Arkansas border, was organized in 1837, but there was still land for homesteading there in 1890. In the 1890s, Riley Adams became the first teacher in the Kentucky Hollow log school, with its puncheon floor and split-log seats. That school was replaced with a frame building, and at times the enrollment reached one hundred, but the school burned and all that remains is the outline of the rock foundation and the rusting remnants of the building's last metal roof. A path, nearly overgrown, leads down to the creek and a little rock-solid springhouse. The spring still delivers a clear flow of water, just as it did when it quenched the thirst of those long-departed students. The names and dates written on the springhouse door record the families that emigrated from Eastern Kentucky to a remote little hollow in the Ozarks: Combs, Johnson, Albright, David, Horner, Martin, numerous Blairs. Penned on the front of the springhouse is this statement: "Luther Blair was born here September 19, 1891 to Lewis and Susan Blair."

I remember going to Kentucky Hollow with Bill Blair to see the log cabin where he had lived as a boy more than forty years ago. Of all the log cabins, which sent nearly one hundred children to the Kentucky Hollow School, it was the only one still visible. On my second visit, its roof had fallen into disrepair. Once the elements are allowed to enter, these sturdy old cabins quickly disintegrate, if they are not already ravaged by the once prevalent woods fires.

Heading down the creek, I wondered at the scant evidence of a once vibrant community: three homes, a springhouse, the rotting log cabin, the rubble of the old school, and the narrow little bottom along the timeless creek, flanked on each side by steep, wooded hillsides. Barely one hundred yards wide at the school site, the valley widens gradually in the two miles or so back to the highway. I forded the creek twice on low water bridges and then I was back at the highway and at the end of Kentucky Hollow. The stream continues across the bottomlands to its union with Beaver Creek, perhaps a mile further. Nearby I once attended a baptising service at a traditional spot on Beaver Creek. It was a joyous occasion, as several small churches initiated those who had accepted Jesus Christ by immersing them in the clear waters.

Then the question I had failed to ask on my previous visits to Kentucky Hollow hit me. I headed back toward Bradleyville to find Bill Blair. A school, a few houses, and a handful of businesses in the midst of a community that still lives by working timber and raising cattle —that is Bradleyville. I found Blair in "Billy Jack's Pkg. Store & Chain Saw Repair."

"So you've been back to Kain-Tuck Holler," he said. "I ain't been back since I took you thet time. Yeah, I heared the old house was falling down."

Bill was wrestling a big chain saw with a collapsed fuel line. "Shore, there's a cemetery in Kain-Tuck Holler. Hit's on the other road."

I had explored the only road I knew all the way to its end, but another further down the highway leads into the upper stretches of the hollow. There I found the Kentucky Hollow burying ground, overgrown with greenbriers, grapevines, briers, and small trees which had reclaimed the spot since the last cemetery working. Presumably, that was sometime around the last burial: Elnora Mannon died July 7, 1972 at the age of 74 years 7 months 27 days, and Thea Mannon died three years earlier at the age of 94. Other recognizable death dates retreated rapidly back into Kentucky Hollow's heyday: 1948, 1936, 1922, 1911, 1901. A number of stones no longer bore dates — if they ever had — being merely creek-smoothed rocks chosen for their appropriate size and shape to mark the final resting place of a loved one.

This meager evidence of a once thriving community is supplemented by the memories of people like Emmett Adams, who fortunately has written of Kentucky Hollow's school, post office, general store, preachers, teachers, blacksmiths and others. Self-sufficiency was the order of the day, and there were even those who pulled teeth, although Adams hesitated to call them dentists. The people lived on farms and produced practically all of their own food and much of their own clothing with the exception of shoes.

The pattern by which Kentucky Hollow was settled was set in Eastern Kentucky and before that in Virginia and North Carolina. Those who were attracted by free or cheap land and willing to wrest a living from rocky hills tilled a few acres, raised some livestock and poultry, gardened, worked in the woods, hunted, and managed to get by. With few exceptions, they raised large families. When the supply of available land grew short in Virginia, there were plenty of immigrants to Kentucky and, subsequently, to the Ozarks. In Kentucky Hollow, the pattern was broken. The frontier had already passed the Ozarks, and there were no more eighty-acre or even forty-acre tracts on which to move. In a generation or two, Kentucky Hollow's prosperity was past, and with no new land to settle, most people dispersed into the country as a whole and into vastly diverse life-styles.

But not entirely. Early settlers of Kentucky Hollow would probably still be at home around Bradleyville, for people there still raise cattle and gardens and work in sawmills or in the timber, albeit with chain saws rather than crosscuts. They are good neighbors. They follow many of the old customs and traditions, and their speech patterns are familiar at Billy Jack's, where they step in to get a saw repaired or to purchase beverages that used to be brewed at home or distilled in the backwoods.

OZARK ATTRACTIONS

The eastern end of Taney County is quite a different story. Tourism received its first impetus early in the twentieth century when Harold Bell Wright's novel, *The Shepherd of the Hills,* was published, and the first railroad opened up the White River Valley. While the train brought a trickle of visitors from the start, a series of other factors have turned the trickle into a torrent.

With the completion of Powersite Dam on the White River, Lake Taneycomo, the first of the Ozarks' man-made lakes, brought vacationers and fishermen to Rockaway Beach, Forsyth, and Branson. The School of the Ozarks, which was founded at Forsyth and later moved to Point Lookout, near Branson, filled a void by providing a high school education for students from isolated communities and by allowing students to pay for their education by working. When needs changed, the school became a junior college. Today it is a four year college which still adheres to the earn-as-you-learn concept. In 1952, Bull Schoals Lake, a project of the U.S. Army Corps of Engineers, impounded eighty miles of the Old White River, downstream from Powersite, and Table Rock Dam, also a Corps project, cre-

Bracket fungi festoon a rotting stump in Devil's Den State Park in Washington County, Arkansas. Some species are destructive parasites of living trees; a few, including the beefsteak mushroom, are prized as food by foragers. Gathering food from the wilds has persisted in the Ozarks from pre-historic times to the present.

"Make do or do without" was the dictum of early Ozark settlers, so scraps were used in making quilts. Quilting skills have survived, and quilts have become an art form. Alice Sego, a native of Winona, Missouri, makes tiny stitches by hand in a cultural demonstration sponsored by the Ozark National Scenic Riverways at Big Spring, on the Current River near Van Buren.

ated another large impoundment just above the headwaters of Lake Taneycomo.

There were three lakes and an imaginative college which had a nationwide following of supporters, but it remained for the families of two men to make the greatest impact on the area. Dr. Bruce Trimble purchased the old homestead which was the setting of *The Shepherd of the Hills*, and Hugo Herschend leased nearby Marvel Cave. Both men died before their dreams could come to fruition, but their widows, both named Mary and both now deceased, proved to be the stuff of which legends are made. Mary Herschend and her sons, Jack and Peter, developed the 1880s-style Silver Dollar City, an entertainment complex featuring arts, crafts, music, and theme park rides above Marvel Cave. Today, Silver Dollar City hosts two large craft festivals, a music festival, and almost 1.5 million customers each year. Mary Trimble and her son, Mark, made Shepherd of the Hills Farm a tourist mecca of similar magnitude and the site of the largest outdoor drama in America, where a quarter of a million people see Wright's story reenacted each year.

Out of these developments rose another phenomenon. The Baldknobbers, a homespun country music show featuring four Mabe brothers, struggled for an audience in an old building on Branson's lakefront for several years. Then another Ozark musical family, that of Lloyd Presley, built Mountain Music Theatre on the highway leading from Branson to Shepherd of the Hills Farm and Silver Dollar City, and the Baldknobbers soon followed suit. Drawn by the lakes, by Silver Dollar City, by Shepherd of the Hills Farm, and by other attractions, the crowds made the new music shows an almost instant success.

Today, there are more than twenty shows, mainly featuring country music and lowbrow comedy styled to family audiences. Encompassing a swatch of the Ozarks from Springfield, Missouri, to the Arkansas line and centered on Branson and Silver Dollar City, "Ozark Mountain Country" has thirty-three thousand entertainment show seats, seven thousand lodging units, and forty-six hundred camping units. Add to this a plethora of restaurants, snack shops, gift shops, and other amusements and attractions. Moreover, immediately to the south of this area is Eureka Springs, Arkansas, with seven thousand entertainment seats and two thousand lodging units.

A startling contrast to nearby communities such as Bradleyville, where the old way of life seems largely undisturbed, this intensely developed tourist area is anathema to many environmentalists and conservationists. But it is a boon to employment and economic development, and the values of the old Ozarks are alive in the glitter of the Branson "strip."

Peter Engler, proprietor of a popular Branson shop, and his late mother, Ida Engler, nurtured Ozark woodcarving. As a result, hundreds of Ozarks people earn all or part of their living from wood sculpture or carving. Bob Mabe, who left the country music show he founded with his brothers to start his own Bob-O-Links Country Music Hoe-Down, is acutely aware of his roots. People like Lloyd and Mollie Heller helped start the Shepherd of the Hills pageant and then launched enterprises providing outlets for performers and craftsmen. During the tourist season, the Mountaineer Book Shop features regional literature in Mutton Hollow, a reconstructed village in the valley below Inspiration Point, where Harold Bell Wright wrote. These institutions offer atmosphere and value which seem in keeping with the Ozark heritage, but the ultimate determiner of success or failure for this welter of enterprise is the buying public.

Mark Trimble, owner of the Shepherd of the Hills Farm, invites competition under the theory that, "What's good for the community is good for the individual." He publishes an Ozark entertainment guide which presents not only Shepherd of the Hills Farm, the Old Mill Theatre, and his Fantastic Caverns and Ozarks Auto Show, but scores of other attractions from Springfield, Missouri, to Eureka Springs, Arkansas. "The more things there are to see and do," declares Trimble, "the more people we are likely to have."

OZARK CHARACTER

On a pleasant side road between Branson and Bradleyville lives Elmo Ingenthron, a local historian who is interested in both communities. Unofficially a stockman, forester, folklorist, conservationist, archaeologist, and agronomist, professionally Ingenthron was a teacher and school administrator. It was unusual for anyone from the one-room rural school he attended to go on to high school, but Elmo went to Branson and received his diploma. Without any college training, he qualified to become a teacher in a rural school and earned forty dollars a month for an eight-month term. He pursued his own education while teaching and eventually earned degrees at Southwest Missouri State and the University of Missouri. After serving as the principal of Branson High School and the superintendent of two other school systems, he was county superintendent of schools for fourteen crucial years, when the far-flung rural schools were consolidated. Ingenthron is particularly proud that the remote hill country moved in the vanguard of the state's school reorganization.

There was plenty of resistance to abolishing the little white schoolhouses which were the focus of community life since the post-Civil War era. But with patience and understanding, Elmo laid out the case time and again: the children would have the same teachers and books, but they would ride to school on buses rather than walk and they would have hot lunch programs and gymnasiums. One school district would serve in place of many. In time, the reorganization passed handily and was implemented without incident.

In 1933, when he was only twenty-two, Elmo bought the 160 acres where he has since lived. On his teacher's salary, he was able to do little more than pay interest up to and including the years when he became a twenty-one dollar per month sailor in World War II. But he could cut brush and build fence and he followed his father's advice to "stay eternally after it."

The farm was his recreation and exercise after teaching, and he developed some unique ideas. Where others fought red cedar as a weed, Elmo encouraged his cedar with trimming, thinning, and the elimination of competing hardwoods. He was one of the first in his area to sow fescue, after paying $1.60 per pound for seed. Many of his neighbors were leery of the grass, because they had heard that it was poisonous. Elmo concedes that there is some danger from a fungus which infests the grass, but he points out that many more Ozark cattle have starved to death from lack of fescue than have been harmed by eating it.

"Hear you got some of that fescue on your place," one neighbor said. "Hope none of that ever gets on my place." Two years later, Elmo sold him a large quantity of fescue seed. Since Elmo also raised purebred Angus cattle, many farmers with low-grade cattle upgraded their herds with sires purchased from Elmo.

A gentle manner and thoughtful practices made a big impact. Andrew Pickett once said, "I learned more about farming looking over Elmo Ingenthron's fence than I did any other way." Elmo's stand of red cedar was judged one of the best in Missouri, and both the Corps of Engineers and the University of Missouri School of Forestry have studied his methods. The school maintains comparative test plots for studying cedar growth on his land.

While he was at home with a chain saw and brush hog, Elmo made himself a scholar. He was aware of earlier Indian cultures from artifacts found around springs, in fresh-plowed bottom fields, and in bluff shelters. The common practice, then and now, was to hunt for perfect specimens and ignore the rest. Elmo,

however, made site collections, carefully detailing the locations, depths, and vital data of every arrowhead, tool, utensil, and fragment he found. Aware of the relocation of Eastern Indians to and through the Ozarks, he also understood the hardships and trials of the early settlers, the devastation of the Civil War, and the War's bitter aftermath.

But there was precious little written on these subjects. Bits and pieces on the Ozarks' two big Civil War battles existed, but there was scant information on scores of other skirmishes and encounters. So Elmo pored through old newspaper files, gleaned references, discovered unpublished diaries, and interviewed the descendants of families which had played a role in the Ozarks' early history.

The first of Elmo's books, *Indians of the Ozark Plateau,* was published by the School of the Ozarks Press in 1970, and *The Land of Taney,* ostensibly a county history but actually an overview of the history of the Ozarks, followed four years later. The third volume in Elmo's Ozark Regional History series, *Borderland Rebellion,* was published in 1980 under the auspices of *The Ozarks Mountaineer.* A retired commercial artist from Aurora, Missouri, Harold Hatzfeld, joined this labor of love. Harold illustrated Elmo's books and accomplished wonders on a meager pension as he helped found the Forsyth Art Guild and sparked the interests of dozens of fledgling artists.

A memory evocative of the man and the Ozarks dates from a fall evening in 1967. We had just moved into a house which contained a fireplace, so after dark Elmo pulled into our driveway in a pick-up loaded with wood. It was not pretty wood, but it was dry and welcome, and he would accept no pay for it. Wood is abundant in the Ozarks, and when you cut and use it Elmo's way, there is no danger of waste or running out. He concentrates on dead and damaged trees and on thinning inferior trees to make more room for others.

Elmo Ingenthron has many distinctive traits which I equate with the best qualities of Ozark people. Perhaps the most unusual in this age is lack of greed. If he sells something, he gives extra measure. If he performs a service, he makes sure he gives full value, and he may not charge at all. "Never get the last nickel out of anything," is his advice.

I have encountered the same trait countless times among Ozark people: the repairman who accepts no pay until you try out the chain saw, garden tiller, or lawn mower to see if it is working properly; the restaurant or cafe that adds a helping of fresh-sliced tomatoes or apple cobbler to your plate-lunch at no extra charge; the hardware store owner who spends twenty minutes

Schoolhouse of a century or more ago on the grounds of the Ozark Folk Center seems ready for students to appear. The Center, an Arkansas state park at Mountain View, works to perpetuate the rich heritage of traditional life in the Ozarks. Crafts and skills dating from 1820 to 1920 are featured, as are pre-1940s music, lyrics, and instruments. Workshops and special events fill the April to October season.

No Niagara to be sure, but these falls at Natural Dam in western Arkansas have been every bit as memorable for generations of swimmers and picnickers. Much of the Lee Creek watershed lies in the Ozark National Forest; the creek itself winds into Oklahoma, and turns southeast to join the Arkansas River near Fort Smith.

helping you find the right nuts and bolts although the sale nets him only a few cents.

One winter's night a few years ago, I was headed home from Springfield over a highway suddenly glazed with ice and snow. I made it over the first of a series of long hills and was headed up the second when the car in front of me spun out. There was traffic coming down the hill, so I had no choice but to let off the gas. Once stopped, I could not get going again, and there was a string of cars stalled all the way up the hill. At that moment I saw a four-wheel-drive truck approach the most distant vehicle, stop, hook on, and pull it to the top. The process was repeated over and over, and by the time my turn came I had inspected my wallet to see if I had enough money to pay. They gave me a pull, and when they unhooked at the top I said, "What do I owe you?" The reply was, "Nothing. We're not doing it for money."

Our family doctor fits the same mold. An Ohio native fresh out of osteopathic school, Bill Roston came to Forsyth seventeen years ago and took over the office of a legendary physician, the late Dr. Theodore Threadgill. Doc Roston quickly became something of a legend himself. He took no appointments, saw patients in his office in the order in which they appeared, and charged three dollars for office calls, a fee which he did not always collect. Doc Roston also made house calls, often driving twenty or thirty miles over back roads, occasionally ruining a tire. What he may have lacked in bedside manner, he more than compensated for with his expertise as a diagnostician.

Bob Spotswood, the pharmacist in Doc's clinic, was every bit as accommodating. Perpetually friendly, he took an interest in everyone and never seemed to tire of filling special needs and going the extra mile for his customers. That sort of spirit seems to be contagious in the Ozarks.

Would Elmo have done so well and accomplished so much if he had followed his contemporaries and succeeding generations and sought his fortune outside the Ozarks? By taking apparently worthless land and making it productive, he has increased his net worth considerably. Moreover, his methods are imitated all over the region, and his contributions to education, recorded history, and folklore are invaluable. He helped to preserve the Ozarks, including its character-rich stories.

One story involved a Taney County farmer who spotted a crippled deer crossing his pasture and killed the deer. The farmer later explained that he was planning to take it into town and turn it over to the game warden, but he had been caught with the carcass and he was hauled into court. The case seemed solid: he admitted to killing the deer. Nevertheless, the jury found him not guilty. An incredulous observer asked a juror how they could find the man not guilty when he "owned up" to killing the deer.

"Well, it's kinda like this," the juror explained. "The judge instructed us that we could believe all or any part of any witness's testimony. We figured the man was just braggin' about the whole thing."

Another unassuming exemplar of generosity was Fred Schmickle. A quiet man, he wrote articles for *The Mountaineer*, took photographs, sold ads, read proofs, tied bundles, and hoisted mail sacks until two days before his death at age eighty-seven. He was always thankful for whatever pay was available, and the closest he ever came to a complaint occurred during the course of a hot, grueling day mailing the magazine. "Oh, to be seventy-five again," he said.

There were many others. The late Edsel Ford gave up a promising journalism career to become a noted northwest Arkansas poet and *The Mountaineer's* poetry columnist:

A poet should die in the country, where the trees
Will bend to touch their fingertips to his,

Where all the flowers that ever bloomed can make
A balm of sweetness to relieve his ache,

Where men of simple ways can walk and feel
A Champion of their faith is with them still,

Where lesser animals can come and know
That here was one who never found them so,

Where each of nature's elements may fall
In tribute to a man who was them all....

—Edsel Ford,
"The Manchild From Sunday Creek."
Copyright 1956, The Kaleidograph Press

For many years Ford was the unpaid publicist of the War Eagle Fair. In fact, most of his endeavors were unpaid or ill paid at best, but he gained for this "cow-pasture exposition" of arts and crafts national publicity. Another writer, Dorothy Mitchell, a transplanted Chicagoan who put her roots in a rocky hilltop near Rogers, Arkansas, also wrote an article on the first fifteen years of the fair and its beginnings at a remote northwest Arkansas crossroads in 1953.

ARTS AND CRAFTS

When a handweavers' guild held a short course at the home of Lester and Blanche Elliott, they found the setting idyllic. An old mill pond was fed by the beautiful War Eagle River which coursed through a wide valley surrounded by hills and covered with pine and hardwood forests. Its huge pine logs hewn by a pioneer named Sylvanus Blackburn in 1832, the Elliotts' home was one of very few in the Ozarks to survive the Civil War. The rest of the structure, added on through the years, became a lodge and restaurant before the Elliotts took up residence.

The original weaving course generated so much enthusiasm that an exhibition was held and other artists and crafts people were invited to show and sell. As the roads to War Eagle consisted of dirt and gravel, and the closest sizeable town was twenty miles away, expectations were not great. But surprisingly, there were three dozen exhibitors and 2,259 guests.

Since then, the War Eagle Fair has been held every year. It has grown to five hundred exhibitors and an estimated one hundred thousand visitors for three days beginning on the third Friday in October. There is no charge for parking or admission, and cars and people fill the valley to its capacity.

Blanche Elliott, now in her eighties and executive director of the fair since its inception, has insisted on keeping the fair free to the public and tightly restricted to high quality arts and crafts from what she calls the four Ozark states—Arkansas, Kansas, Missouri, and Oklahoma. Commissions and booth fees paid by exhibitors at the Fall Fair and an Antique and Heritage Craft Show held at the same location the first weekend in May allow the non-profit Ozarks Arts and Crafts Fair Association to sponsor an annual arts and crafts seminar in mid-June and to contribute to scholarships and historical preservation projects.

The Fair's impact is immense. Sales total about half a million dollars, and, with every motel and restaurant in northwest Arkansas filled to capacity, the amount of money generated runs rapidly into the millions.

On the same October weekend, a dozen or more arts and crafts events take place in the vicinity. They range in size from yard and parking lot setups to the Bella Vista Arts and Crafts Festival, which rivals War Eagle in every respect. Bella Vista, a retirement development twenty-five miles away, has a well-organized volunteer group which manages the show and operates an arts and crafts shop the rest of the year.

The War Eagle Fair retains historical preeminence, but the five-week-long "National Festival of Craftsmen" at Silver Dollar City surpasses it in sales. Arts and crafts events occur somewhere in the Ozarks virtually every weekend from April into October, and the number of shops featuring arts and crafts made in the Ozarks has increased dramatically and is still growing.

Gene and Ellen Pendergraft came to the Ozarks from Texas and established their mountaintop gallery for regionally produced arts and crafts along Scenic Highway 7, south of Jasper, Arkansas. With the works of two hundred Missourians and Arkansans, Pendergraft Arts and Crafts is a continuing show from April through Thanksgiving. Although they are a two-hour drive from War Eagle, the weekend of the War Eagle Fair is usually their year's biggest.

The War Eagle Fair provided the impetus for the arts and crafts movement in the Ozarks. The Arkansas-wide Ozark Foothills Craft Guild, based in Mountain View, operates five shops and hosts three important fairs each year. Scores of individuals and organizations such as the Ozark Native Craft Association of Winslow, Arkansas, nourish the movement. They have all derived inspiration from War Eagle.

Folk music has undergone a similar revival in the Ozarks, although the economic impact is far less. There are thousands of people earning all or part of their livelihood from arts and crafts, while only a few hundred gain any income from folk music. But folk music is thriving, thanks in large measure to the establishment of the Ozark Folk Center at Mountain View, Arkansas, and to such events as the Original Ozark Folk Festival in Eureka Springs, Arkansas, which dates back to 1948.

Today, Mountain View includes: the Ozark Folk Center with its regular folk music programs, the Jimmy Driftwood Theatre featuring the Rackensack Folklore Society, the Mountain View Folklore Society which performs on the courthouse lawn in summer and in their own hall in winter, the Grandpa Jones Dinner Theater, and a coffeehouse featuring folk music. Yet not surprisingly, some of the best folk music is played in living rooms and on porches, all over the Ozarks; and a number of localities, such as Salem, Arkansas, have regularly scheduled folk music sessions which are free to the public.

Best known for music, the Ozark Folk Center is run by the State of Arkansas and features crafts and folkways. Folk musicians Bobby and Kay Blair perform at the Center and fill important roles there as well: Kay directs crafts, while Bobby is a nature guide and beekeeper and demonstrates pioneer skills. In the woods he is an expert hunter, trapper, and forager. He once "coursed" a hive of bees, then led a party to harvest the wild honey. A lean, angular man, he seems a throwback to the Ozarkers of a hundred years ago.

With his collections of songs, music, and tales, Bill McNeil of the Ozark Folk Center bids fair to becoming the region's second great folklorist. The first was the

Reflections of fall foliage color the Black River at Johnson Shut-Ins. The river's East Fork is constricted in width and steepened where it cuts through the resistant igneous rock. One of the Ozarks' favorite natural attractions, the Johnson Shut-Ins State Park is fourteen miles Southwest of Ironton, Missouri.

Bluffs ring the summit of White Rock Mountain in the Ozark National Forest west of Cass, Arkansas. From the lookout shelter on the far bluff, the lights of Fort Smith, Arkansas, and Tulsa, Oklahoma, are visible on clear evenings.

late Vance Randolph. A native of Pittsburg, Kansas, Vance fell in love with the Ozarks at the age of seven, when his family vacationed in Noel, Missouri. Carl Sandburg put him on the trail of regional folklore, and Vance, who took up permanent residence in the Ozarks while in his twenties, stayed on the trail for nearly sixty years.

Vance wrote twenty books, ranging from little books on ghost stories and tall tales to the four volume collection of nine hundred ballads and songs, *Ozark Folksongs*. He studied every aspect of Ozark life and lived it, participating in fishing trips, fox hunts, baptisings, barroom brawls, backwoods dances, moonshine drinking bouts, turkey shoots and, as his friend Ernie Deane wrote, "every other imaginable kind of activity involving mountain people." He supported himself by writing his books and newspaper and magazine articles. His most profitable volume, *Pissing in the Snow and Other Ozark Folk Tales*, is a collection of bawdy stories. It was assembled through the years, as Ernie Deane reported, by "a man absolutely dedicated to his life's mission of bringing together in an orderly way uncounted thousands of bits of information about the Ozarks and their people."

THE WATERS

After private interests had dammed the White River at Powersite in 1913 and the Osage River at Bagnell in the early 1930s, the U.S. Army Corps of Engineers finished Norfork Dam and Lake on the North Fork of the White River in 1943, Bull Shoals Dam and Lake in 1952, Table Rock Dam and Lake in 1958, and Beaver Dam and Lake in 1964. Virtually all of the upper White River was impounded.

In the eastern Missouri Ozarks, two smaller lakes, Wappapello and Clearwater, were created. Also in southwest Missouri, Pomme de Terre Lake, Stockton Lake, and Truman Lake impounded the Pomme de Terre, Sac, and Upper Osage rivers respectively. In Arkansas, a dam on the Little Red River created Greers Ferry Lake.

In 1965, the Arkansas River was dammed at Dardanelle. Eastern Oklahoma acquired the big reservoirs of Grand Lake of the Cherokees, Fort Gibson, and Tenkiller Ferry. And in the southwestern Arkansas Ouachitas, extensive Lake Ouachita near Hot Springs was joined by lesser impoundments such as Lakes Blue Mountain, Nimrod, Maumelle, Hinkle, Wilhelmina, and Hamilton.

With many projects afoot in 1965, conservationists worried that the Corps was out to dam every free-flowing stream in the Ozarks. Built with the objectives of flood control and electric power generation, the lakes were even more conspicuous for their recreational uses. Equally important, they spurred tourism and economic development.

But the conservationists argued that in creating the lakes something even more valuable was lost. The Ozark Society, a conservationist group styled after the national Sierra Club, led the effort to save the Buffalo River. The conservationists won a fight, which was emotional and at times bitter, through an educational program capped by the publication of Kenneth Smith's fine book, *Buffalo River Country*. Brought under the aegis of the National Park Service, the Buffalo River is now preserved in its beautiful and natural state.

Spearheaded by Leonard Hall's book, *Stars Upstream*, a drive to preserve the Current and Jack's Fork rivers in the Ozark National Scenic Riverways preceded the Buffalo River battle. A last-ditch effort blocked dams on the Meramec River, and conservationists effectively halted other proposed dams on Ozark streams. Presumably, the Ozarks now has all the big lakes it is going to have for the foreseeable future. Efforts to the contrary would surely bring back "Dam the Corps of Engineers" bumper stickers.

One year, Larry Price and I floated from the ghost mining town of Rush, Arkansas, to the mouth of the Buffalo with a group from the Ozark Society. We were fledgling floaters. Our canoe contained an ice chest full of food, sleeping bags, and a package of big plastic bags, the kind used for leaves.

We paddled all day, drinking in the wildly beautiful scenery, and made camp that night with our companions on a gravel bar. They popped out colorful little tents and prepared freeze-dried food. We ate much better, positioned our sleeping bags in a sandy spot, and went to sleep looking at the stars. Sometime in the early morning, we were awakened by a clap of thunder and felt rain starting to fall. We found our plastic bags, slit them open and draped them over poles we leaned against small trees. We secured the ends of the bags with rocks and pushed our sleeping bags inside the improvised lean-tos, but it really poured, and by dawn's early light we had sprung several leaks.

Larry and I each cut holes for arms and heads in a plastic bag, pulled on our "ponchos," and started a fire on which we fried ham and eggs. Our companions had stayed drier, but they were willing to acknowledge the superiority of our fare and joined us for breakfast. We had to be the sorriest-looking campers that ever floated the Buffalo, but I would not want my children or grandchildren to miss that experience.

THE CITIES

The cities of the Ozarks are an important part of the region and rather unique, too. Consider Springfield, Missouri, the "Queen City of the Ozarks." I do not know the origin of that nickname, but it is appropriate. By far the largest Ozark city, with more than one hundred and fifty thousand people, Springfield somehow manages to be just a big country town. It has a goodly share of industry, but more importantly, it provides goods and services for millions of people living in southwest Missouri and northwest Arkansas. A major center for hospitals and medical services, Springfield is home to Southwest Missouri State University and four other colleges. Ozark people focus on Springfield. They say, "I'll get it when I go to Springfield," confidently and comfortably.

Much the same is true of the northwest Arkansas cities of Fayetteville-Springdale-Rogers, if you consider them as one big city. The University of Arkansas is located in Fayetteville, and there are excellent medical facilities, a number of industries, and the goods and services which create a trade center. More on the perimeter of the region, Joplin and Poplar Bluff, Missouri, and Fort Smith, Arkansas, fill similar roles. All are big country towns, made considerably bigger by what they provide to outlying areas. In the Ozark heartland, smaller cities also serve as trade centers, though on a smaller scale. With their populations ranging between five thousand and ten thousand, Lebanon and West Plains, Missouri, and Harrison and Batesville, Arkansas, are notable examples.

For most of the Ozarks, population peaked about 1900 and declined for the following fifty years. Then the trend reversed, and population growth began again, although not in the same patterns created by the early settlers. A major factor is the discovery of the Ozarks by retired people. The creation of the big lakes contributed, witness the number of retirees living in Mountain Home, Heber Springs, Fairfield Bay, Rogers, and Eureka Springs, Arkansas, and in Forsyth, Branson, Shell Knob, and Lake of the Ozarks, Missouri. Kimberling City, Missouri, had its birth with the formation of Table Rock Lake, and retired people are the backbone of its thriving community.

Retirement developments have created cities at Cherokee Village, Bella Vista, and Horseshoe Bend in Arkansas, while locations such as Cassville, Missouri, and Jasper, Arkansas, lure retirees with their natural attractions and Ozark life-style. The contribution retired people make to the Ozarks is inestimable. They fill voids in knowledge and service, take up arts and crafts, contribute to community service, start businesses, and increase the region's vitality.

RELIGION

People seem to feel a special way in the Ozarks, and much is made of the Ozarks as a stronghold of fundamentalist Christianity. Perhaps a statistical case can be made, but the relationship of man with his Maker is not confined by denominational ties. The international headquarters of the Assemblies of God is in Springfield, but the city recently saw a former citizen become the archbishop of Boston, one of the nation's largest Catholic communities. Moveover, many religious people are not affiliated with any organized religion. Instead, they echo Jimmy Driftwood's song, "My church is under the trees..."

Eureka Springs, Arkansas, presents some interesting contrasts. Originally a spa noted for the healing qualities of its water, it is a booming tourist town with gift and antique shops, country music shows, and other attractions. But Eureka Springs is also the place where the late Gerald L. K. Smith built the seven-story-high Christ of the Ozarks statue and established a Passion Play. At the time the controversial Smith built the statue, *Time Magazine* suggested he was building a personal monument, but Smith is dead, and people continue to come by the thousands every year to see the statue and the play.

South of Eureka Springs is Hillspeak, the headquarters of the Episcopal Book Club and *The Anglican Digest* magazine, and on yet another hilltop rises the architecturally stunning Thorncrown Chapel, a nondenominational place of worship. In Eureka Springs stands the Catholic St. Elizabeth's Church, once featured in Ripley's *Believe It Or Not* as the church that is entered through its bell tower. Diverse? Yes. Inspired? Yes. That is religion in the Ozarks.

OUTLYING REGIONS

There are some fascinating outlying regions of the Ozarks. One which has always piqued my interest is Crowley's Ridge. Shaped like a late moon, it arcs two hundred miles south from Cape Girardeau, Missouri, to Helena, Arkansas. It is surmised that the Mississippi River's ancient streambeds account for the flat alluvial plains on either side of Crowley's Ridge, which varies in width from twenty miles to a few hundred feet. Usually five to ten miles wide, Crowley's Ridge looks like the Ozarks. Without the influence of the rich flatlands on either side, the ridge, which afforded a

Rag-rug is woven on a loom in Eureka Springs. Some twenty-five miles to the south is the remote hamlet of War Eagle, where the Northwest Arkansas Handweavers Guild held a workshop followed by an exhibit in 1953. So was born the War Eagle Fair, which has inspired intense interest in arts and crafts in the Ozarks. The free-admission, three-day fair on the third weekend in October has annual sales of nearly a half million dollars.

Luke Jeter, a two-time state and national fiddler, plays for a community musical at Beaver, Arkansas. Traditional and folk music have strong roots in the Ozarks. Held in many Missouri and Arkansas communities, weekly musicals are usually quite informal and many are free of charge. Beaver is on the old White River, just downstream from Beaver Lake and on the upper reaches of Table Rock Lake.

route into the lowlands and a base for draining the swamps, would be culturally indistinguishable from the region.

The disorientation on Crowley's Ridge is quickly cured by looking out over the lowlands on either side. At some places, such as Dexter, Missouri, it is possible to see flat country to both the east and the west. But the Arkansas Valley and the Ouachita Mountains to the south of the Ozarks offer no easy dividing line, although geologically there is a difference. Milton Rafferty speaks of "the tightly folded and strongly faulted rocks of the Arkansas Valley and Ouachita Mountains." Friedrich Gerstacker, who traveled in the Ouachitas in 1844 and was a German counterpart to Henry Schoolcraft, wrote:

The hills and rivers south of the Arkansas almost run, like that river, from west to east, and the hills have a peculiar formation. The middle row or back-bone ridge is the highest, and generally on either side are two or three lower ranges of hills, running parallel to the main range, and sloping more and more towards the plain. All the smaller rivers which run into the Arkansas from this side have such hills between them.

I understand this just as I understand the unique features of Potato Hill Mountain in Yell County or the highest point in all the Interior Highlands, Mount Magazine in Logan County, but if you blindfolded me before I crossed the Arkansas River, I would still not know whether I was in the Boston Mountains, the Arkansas Valley, or the Ouachitas. To a layman, the mountains are unique but no more unique than Big Pilot in the Hercules Glade Wilderness of Taney County, Missouri. In short, it all looks like Ozarks to me, and apparently it did to Vance Randolph, too.

Many of Vance's books contain songs and stories gleaned from the Ouachitas. Mena, Arkansas, was particularly productive for his collections. A Mena businessman once told Vance, "'It got so dry there one summer that my office girl had to fasten stamps on envelopes with a stapler. It's so dry here right now,' he said earnestly, 'that the cottonmouths carry little vials of water, to prime themselves before they can spit cotton.'" Vance later explained, "This gentleman and I belong to the same lodge," so he gave him a drink of the bottle in his briefcase.

Vance also described the impact of the radio comedians Lum and Abner: "Their hillbilly heaven was really the village of Waters, in Montgomery County, Arkansas, but they called it Pine Ridge on the air. The people of Waters recognized their local characters in the Lum and Abner program and had sense enough to take advantage of this free publicity. Realizing that their backwardness was a commercial asset, the villagers put DRIVE KEERFUL signs and others calculated to catch the eye of the 'furrin' motorist. Almost immediately tourists were swarming all over the place, and the residents made good money by being picturesque and selling souvenirs." Eventually, the name of the town was officially changed to Pine Ridge. Apparently a lot of people share a trait with Vance and me: they cannot tell the Ozarks from the Ouachitas.

There is plenty that is distinctive and unusual in the Ouachitas. Consider Hot Springs. A number of towns in the region received their initial impetus as spas. Eureka Springs, Heber Springs, and Sulphur Springs in Arkansas and El Dorado Springs, Ponce De Leon, and Siloam Springs in Missouri — all had waters which were thought to have curative or restorative powers. But most of these towns have gone on to other things, or, in the case of the latter two, they have lapsed into anonymity. In contrast, Hot Springs, which was known to the Indians as the "Valley of Vapors," was set aside as a reservation in 1832 and became a national park in 1921. Today, its 1,035 acres include forty-seven thermal springs, five scenic mountains, and Bathhouse Row, where travelers from around the world bathe in its therapeutic waters.

Three lakes follow the meandering Ouachita River. Arkansas Power and Light Company built the first two — Lake Catherine in 1924 and Lake Hamilton in 1931. By far the largest is Lake Ouachita, a Corps of Engineers project backing up fifty-two miles behind Blakely Mountain Dam, which was dedicated in 1956. Only twenty-nine miles to the south is DeGray Reservoir on the Caddo River, and to the west lies Lake Greeson, an impoundment of the Little Missouri River. Both are Corps of Engineers projects, opened in 1972 and 1950 respectively.

The city of Hot Springs was incorporated in 1876 and features a panoply of other attractions in addition to the national park: eleven weeks of thoroughbred horse racing begin in early February at Oaklawn Park; Magic Springs Theme Park, the Arkansas Fun Festival, and music and theater kick off the summer, followed by an annual Oktoberfest. But for all of its attractions and diversions, a major part of the charm of Hot Springs, like Branson and Eureka Springs, is its proximity to the seclusion and wilderness of the surrounding, heavily forested hills. There are a million and a half acres in the Ouachita National Forest, so a person could spend several lifetimes seeing it all, and botanists in particular love the flora growing among those east-west ridges in the sheer vastness of rolling woodlands.

For those with less time, the Talimena Scenic Drive is a particular favorite in the spring, when dogwood is in bloom, and in autumn, when the trees don their brilliant colors. The drive extends fifty-four miles from Talihina, Oklahoma, to Mena, Arkansas. Established in 1970, Talimena is a National Forest Service project free of billboards and other man-made obstructions. Going west from Mena in a steep climb over the mountains, there are twenty-two scenic overlooks spaced over twelve miles.

The drive also brings the traveler to Queen Wilhelmina State Park. Built there by a railroad company in the late 1800s, the picturesque inn was named for the young queen of Holland. In time, the inn fell into disuse, was sold at auction, and was then replaced by a new structure constructed by the Arkansas State Parks Division.

The second inn burned in 1973, and the state erected an impressive wood, glass, and native stone lodge, but the view of the Ouachitas from this lodge is even more spectacular. There are thirty-eight guest rooms, a restaurant, and meeting room. A miniature railroad carries visitors through part of the park, and there are guided hikes and nature programs in summer. The park is open year-round, and a portion of the two hundred-mile-long Ouachita Hiking Trail passes through it.

Each person who visits or lives in the Ozarks or Ouachitas finds his own favorite country: the smoke trees in autumn along the Glade Top Trail near Ava, Missouri, the profusion of dogwoods in spring on Arkansas Highway 9 between Mountain View and Melbourne. The Buffalo, Current, Jacks Fork, and Eleven Point rivers are fine float streams, and there are scores of others in the Interior Highlands. The Ouachita, the Caddo, and the Cossatot rivers provide floating in the Ouachitas, along with many other streams. In dry weather, some streams look like rocky hiking trails, but in wetter times they provide great sport, and after heavy rains they can be dangerous.

Learning is part of living in the Ozarks. Billy Joe Tatum is a physician's wife who found health by becoming an expert on wild plants. She discovered that the key to her mental well-being lay in the outdoors of Izard County and in writing *Wild Foods Cookbook and Field Guide,* although she had never written before. Jim and Barbara Larkin are an example of people who elected to make a go of it as full-time potters, even though they faced college expenses for their children. Anyone who settles in the Ozarks can expect to pay a price for the privilege of living in the region, yet one learns so much. It was true of the early settlers, today's newcomers, and likely for those to come.

This leads us back to the question of what is so special about the Ozarks. I asked the question of Rex Harral of Wilburn, Arkansas, a farmer and craftsman and, more precisely a woodworker and blacksmith.

Rex replied, "The people and their culture and traditions." He went on to talk about the self-sustaining, family-oriented way of life. Rex has lived on his 120 acres for forty-three years, cleared the land, worked in the woods, and built all his buildings. A fountain of information on the old-time skills, he knows how to tan leather, make corncob pipes, and weave hickory bark baskets, among dozens of other skills. He still farms with horses, and a few years ago when his shop burned, he built it back in seven weeks. The only materials that did not come from his place were the nails and roofing. Rex says, "It's like a professor that was traveling through this country one time and met a kid coming back from the grist mill. He had a sack over his shoulder with a pumpkin in one end and the corn meal in the other. The professor asked him why he did that, and the kid replied that that was the way his daddy and granddaddy had done it and that's the way he wanted to do it, too."

Gold from a setting sun tints a hardwood forest's spring leaves on Magazine Mountain. At 2,753 feet above sea level, Magazine Mountain is the highest point in the interior highlands and in the four states of Missouri, Arkansas, Oklahoma, and Kansas. Geologically, the mountain is not part of the Ozarks or the Ouachitas, but belongs to the Arkansas Valley, which lies between the two.

Above: Ozark mushroom hunters begin foraging for prized morels in the spring and may cap a long season with a find of hygrophorus in November. "Yellow sweetbreads" are best eaten fresh but they may be frozen. *Right:* Spring flowers surround deserted home in the Buffalo River Valley. Bluffs along the one hundred and fifty mile-long Buffalo National River provide fine views.

Left: A good fisherman must be eternally optimistic. Only optimism can explain the lone figure in Oklahoma's Sequoyah State Park on Fort Gibson Reservoir just before sunset in October. *Above:* Current-powered ferries were fairly common in the Ozarks a generation or two ago. Now only this ferry on the Current River in Shannon County, Missouri, and a handful of others remain.

Above: Still thriving more than one hundred years after its founding as a spa, Eureka Springs, Arkansas, is called the "Little Switzerland of the Ozarks." Basin Park Hotel on the left was built beside the original healing spring; each of its seven floors has a ground level entrance. *Right:* Spring-fed pond furnishes power for Alley Spring Mill in Shannon County near Eminence, Missouri. *Overleaf:* Thunderstorm gathers force over Table Rock Lake.

Left: Blacksmith's shop with forge at Owl's Bend on the Current River in Missouri is one of many cultural demonstrations sponsored by the National Park Service. The village has had a blacksmith shop since before the Civil War. *Above:* Bruce B. Grimes, a gunsmith in Silver Dollar City, Missouri, shows off .40 caliber rifle with a hand-carved stock. *Overleaf:* White Rock Mountain gives topside view of the Boston Mountains.

Above: Traditional music and crafts are an integral part of the life of Violet Hensley of Yellville, Arkansas. While raising a large family and working, she has found time to participate in festivals, playing fiddles she makes herself. *Right:* Mists hover over cold water and crisp watercress in a branch running from Round Spring into the Current River in Shannon County, Missouri. Part of the Ozark Scenic Riverway, the spring discharges 26 million gallons of water on an average day.

Left: A flume once carried spring water to the huge, overshot wheel of Turners Mill in Oregon County, Missouri. Now the wheel rusts as the waters meander around it en route to the Eleven Point River. *Above:* Ancient bluffs of stoic gray peer through a forest of changing colors in this view to the north of White Rock Mountain. Gum trees are crimson; oaks and hickories range from yellow to brown.

Above: Although it is one of the Ozarks' most popular lakes, Lake of the Ozarks offers a pristine solitude worthy of Northern Canada at Lake of the Ozarks State Park near Brumley, Missouri. *Right:* The lower part of Eden Falls is visible from Cob Cave, as Clark Creek follows an imaginative path through Lost Valley in Newton County, Arkansas, to juncture with the Buffalo River. The cave was dry shelter for Indians who left small corn cobs there.

Left: East of Booneville, Arkansas, Cameron Bluffs form part of Mount Magazine, the highest point in the Interior Highlands, which include the Ozarks and Ouachitas. *Above:* Horse-drawn cultivator in Old Matt's barn on the Shepherd of the Hills Farm near Branson, Missouri. Across Mutton Hollow is Compton Ridge. All of the names are taken from the novel, *Shepherd of the Hills,* which is presented every year as outdoor theater on the farm for which it was named.

Above: Mildred and Jess Lane decorate their homestead between Lampe and Kimberling City, Missouri, with colorful bottles and gourds. *Right:* Alley Spring, near Eminence, Missouri, flows an average 81 million gallons per day and still powers the turbine of the old red mill, where corn is ground on stone buhrs. *Overleaf:* Clear autumn day near the entrance to Ha Ha Tonka State Park in Camden County, Missouri.

Left: Breathtaking view of the Buffalo River. The ledge along Big Bluff, which is called the Goat Trail, is near Ponca, Arkansas. *Above:* Cathedral Room of Marvel Cave compares to the Astrodome in size and has welcomed visitors for a century. Silver Dollar City, which was built above it, has become nationally known. *Overleaf:* Near Current River, large round bales of hay are popular with Ozark cattlemen, who store them in the open where they are fed to cattle.

Above: Meadows near Theodosia in Ozark County, Missouri. Although unsuited to cultivated crops, the rolling and rocky hills of the Ozarks can be quite productive when improved as pastures. *Right:* Also in Ozark County is Dawt Mill, built in 1900 by Master Millwright Alva Hodgson. Still grinding corn, today the mill is powered by a turbine at the end of a millrace where a handmade dam funnels the force of the North Fork River.

Left: Rim of bluff above Hemmed-In-Hollow in the Buffalo National River area of Newton County, Arkansas. A U-shaped, blind canyon, Hemmed-In-Hollow is thought to be the site of a collapsed cave. At the head of the canyon, water pours over a two hundred-foot waterfall, then flows into the Buffalo. *Above:* Colorful fanfare accompanies the changing of the seasons in the Boston Mountains.

Above: The French established Ste. Genevieve, the first permanent settlement west of the Mississippi, about 1735. The Bolduc House was built about 1770. The eroding river bank necessitated moving the town and the Bolduc House. Now authentically restored, the house has stood at its present location for two centuries. *Right:* West of Eureka Springs, Inspiration Point overlooks White River Valley. *Overleaf:* Hills are mirrored in the Meramec River near Meramec Caverns.

Left: Yellowing maples decorate forest at Lake of the Ozarks State Park. *Above:* Major Jacob Wolf, an Indian agent, constructed this grand home in the winter of 1828 and 1829, in sight of the spot where the North Fork flows into the White River at present day Norfork, Arkansas. His great-great-grandniece, Helen Chapman, conducts tours of the Wolf House. *Overleaf:* Blacksmith labors at forge on grounds of the Ozark Folk Center, Mountain View, Arkansas.

Left: The spring-fed waters of Roaring River State Park in Missouri churn a collage of crystal, emerald, and white the year around, but the park's liveliest day is the first of March, when the trout season opens. *Above:* The heart of the business district in Kingston, Arkansas, is deceiving, but the sleepy appearance of small Ozark towns such as this one belies their vigorous community spirit. *Overleaf:* Sunrise on Greenleaf Lake in Muskogee County, Oklahoma.

Above: When Harold Bell Wright was writing *The Shepherd of the Hills,* this cabin was the home of Mr. and Mrs. J. K. Ross. After the book was published in 1908, it became known as Old Matt's Cabin. Although the Rosses had moved to nearby Roark Valley, they were identified as Old Matt and Aunt Mollie. *Right:* Thunderhead towers over the Ozark National Forest south of Pelsor, Arkansas.

Left: Sunset south of Pontiac, Missouri, on Bull Shoals Lake. Wiggling along the border with Arkansas like a giant serpent, the lake isolates the citizens of one state from each other. A long point below Pontiac is part of Arkansas but it is accessible by land only from Missouri. *Above:* Round Spring, a major attraction of Ozark National Scenic Riverways, flows under a natural bridge into the Current River.

Above: "Waste not, want not" were bywords for early Ozark settlers. Corn was a staple in their diet, and the entire plant was used. Demonstrating the old craft of shuckery, Velma Irene Haymes of Conway, Missouri, makes a chair seat out of corn shucks at the National Festival of Craftsmen at Silver Dollar City, Missouri. *Right:* Tenkiller Ferry Reservoir at Tenkiller State Park near Gore, Oklahoma.

Left: The Buffalo River passes by Big Bluff in its crooked path across northern Arkansas. Near Ponca in Newton County, this 500-foot cliff is bisected by Goat Trail, a 350-foot high ledge which narrows at one point to only two yards wide. *Above:* Spring is here for sure when the dogwood blooms, say old-timers. Generally, dogwood blooms about the middle of April, but this may vary by weeks from year to year depending on weather and location.

Above: Mountain View, Arkansas, the folk music capital of the Ozarks the year around, celebrates the Arkansas Folk Festival on an April weekend, and folks come from all over to play and listen. *Right:* Overhanging bluffs provided shelters for the Ozarks' prehistoric residents, the Bluff-dwellers. *Overleaf:* Alum Cove Natural Bridge in the Ozark National Forest between Deer and Parthenon, Arkansas, was used as a bridge by early settlers.

Left: Pedal-pipe organ in a Eureka Springs antique shop displays mementos from the past. *Above:* Barracks, courthouse, and jail complex in Fort Smith, Arkansas, where the "hanging judge," Isaac C. Parker, presided from 1875 to 1896, imposing his interpretation of law on Indian territory. The courtroom and gallows have been restored. *Overleaf:* One of two major Civil War battles in the Ozarks was fought at Pea Ridge, Arkansas, now a national military park.

Above: Large hay bales shed morning dew in a field west of Van Buren, Missouri. Carter County has fewer residents today than in 1900 but boasts more cattle and many more visitors with nearby Big Spring and the Ozark National Scenic Riverways. *Right:* Purple and gold predominate in sunset over Pomme de Terre Lake in Hickory County, Missouri, north of Bolivar.

Left: Clarence Lyons shapes a boat paddle out of sassafras wood. A native whose family moved to the Ozarks from Kentucky in 1898, he builds the traditional flat-bottomed johnboats in a cultural demonstration for the Ozark National Scenic Riverways near Van Buren, Missouri. *Above:* Old cabins, such as these at Ponca, Arkansas, can survive neglect so long as they are protected by roofs.

Above: Near Ponca, Arkansas, the fog-shrouded banks at the confluence of Steele Creek and the Buffalo River provide temporary sanctuary. With spectacular bluffs and good float conditions, the Buffalo River attracts canoeists from many states. *Right:* Quiet morning on the upper Buffalo. After heavy rains the river is transformed into a raging torrent. *Overleaf:* Big Spring, near Van Buren, Missouri, is the largest in the Ozarks. At its maximum flow it is the largest in the nation.

Left: Huzzah Creek in Crawford County, Missouri, after a heavy rain runs full and roaring over the dam at Dillard Mill. *Above:* The Boston Mountains in the Southern Ozarks technically are not really mountains, but they are impressive when seen through morning mist. *Overleaf:* It is not the dogwood's true flower that makes it an Ozark favorite, but the blossom's four petal-like bracts.

Above: Born in Pennyslvania, Lloyd "Shad" Heller is an actor who became a blacksmith. The mayor and spokesman for Silver Dollar City, he has appeared on the *Beverly Hillbillies* and with his wife Ruth runs Wilderness Settlement Craft Village and the Corn Crib Theatre at Branson, Missouri. *Right:* Fishing in Spavinaw Creek, Spavinaw, Oklahoma. *Overleaf:* Quill pens in one-room school at the Ozark Folk Center.

Left: An average 276 million gallons of water a day "boils" out of a jumble of boulders that comprise the wreckage of the orifice of Big Spring in Carter County, Missouri. The water flows about one thousand feet before joining the Current River. *Above:* On December 7, 1862, a village church became a makeshift Confederate hospital in the Civil War battle of Prairie Grove, Arkansas. Casualties for both Union and Confederate soldiers totaled 2,568.

Above: Sunset in the Beaver Dam Recreation Area near Eureka Springs, Arkansas. The uppermost of four dams which impound two hundred miles of the old White River, Beaver Dam was completed, and the lake filled, in 1964. *Right:* Waterfall on nature trail at Devil's Den State Park near Winslow, Arkansas. Other features include Devil's Den Cave, Devil's Ice Box, and bridle and backpacking trails.

Left: Morning fog from a vantage point overlooking Greenleaf Lake, just north of the Arkansas River Navigation System between Gore and Muskogee, Oklahoma. *Above:* Boy uses the last minutes of daylight to fish in the Jacks Fork River near Alley Spring in Ozark National Scenic Riverways. Smallmouth bass are the piscatorial prizes here, but goggle-eye and sunfish are just as good to eat.

Above: Hills around Lost Bridge area of Beaver Lake look cold and lonely when covered with snow, but the lakes have helped reverse a declining trend in population which existed for more than fifty years. Currently, two million people live in the Ozarks. *Right:* Once a center of social activities for officers at nearby Fort Gibson, Murrell House near Tahlequah, Oklahoma, was one of few area homes to survive the Civil War.

Left: Elephant Rocks State Park features a herd of pink granite elephants. Geologists say that they originated as molten rock more than a billion years ago and then cracked and weathered. Located at Graniteville, Missouri, in Iron County, the largest of the herd weighs almost seven hundred tons. *Above:* Falling Spring Mill on Hurricane Creek near the Eleven Point River in Missouri. *Overleaf:* Mt. Olive Church near Boxley, Arkansas.

Above: Sugar Loaf Mountain rises majestically out of Greers Ferry Lake near the resort and retirement community of Fairfield Bay, Arkansas. Dam near Heber Springs backs up waters of the Little Red River. *Right:* Jacks Fork River at Alley Spring near Eminence, Missouri. *Overleaf:* Cove Lake in the Ozark National Forest, ten miles south of Paris, Arkansas, near Magazine Mountain.

Left: The end of another beautiful day on Table Rock Lake near Kimberling City, Missouri. Built at the site of an old ferry-crossing after the lake was completed in 1958, Kimberling City is a great favorite with retirees from adjoining states. *Above:* Free folk music is a tradition on the courthouse lawn in Mountain View, Arkansas. Square is filled for April's Arkansas Folk Festival.

Above: Fourth largest of Missouri's springs, and one of the most highly developed, Bennett Springs in Dallas County, west of Lebanon, is a state park with a trout hatchery, old mill dam, and two miles of creek popular with trout fishermen. *Right:* Fallen leaves form a colorful mosaic in the Hahn State Park in the St. Francois Mountains of Eastern Missouri.

Left: Autumn comes to the Trail of Tears State Park near Cape Girardeau, Missouri. The park was named for the forced march made by the Cherokees from their homelands in the southeast. The trail, on which many died, crossed the Mississippi at this location. *Above:* Federal men pursued corn-whiskey makers in the old days; now Elmer Willie brews whiskey as a National Parks Service demonstration. *Overleaf:* Autumn reflections in the Lake of the Ozarks.

Above: Mississippi River bluffs, looking north from the vicinity of a rocky promontory, which was the 1720 outpost of Ensign Girardot, a Frenchman from Kaskaskia. The permanent settlement of Cape Girardeau, Missouri, came later in the century, long before pioneers settled the interior of the Ozarks. *Right:* Steep, pine-strewn hills east of Eureka Springs, Arkansas. *Overleaf:* The White River flows free past the beautiful bluffs of Calico Rock, Arkansas.

Left: ''Truly primeval,'' is author Kenneth Smith's description of the Buffalo River country around Falling Water Falls. Falling Water Creek runs into Richland Creek, which is a tributary of the Buffalo. *Above:* Time-out for a fly fisherman at Bennett Spring State Park. *Overleaf:* Illinois hills across the Mississippi from Cape Girardeau are called Ozarks by some, but may be continuation of Kentucky Hills.

Above: At remote Haw Creek Falls in the Ozark National Forest, eight campsites are deemed sufficient for an area of exquisite beauty. Accessible only by gravel roads, Haw Creek Falls is located in Crawford County, Arkansas. *Right:* Boat motors are limited to ten horsepower on eighty-two-acre Spring Lake in the Ozark National Forest. The lake is accessible by gravel roads from Dardanelle to the north and Belleville to the south.

Left: Downstream from the confluence of the Jacks Fork and Current rivers near Eminence, Missouri, evening sheds a special light on the Owls Bend area of the Ozark National Scenic Riverways. *Above:* The fiddle is so esteemed that Arkansas designated it the state's official musical instrument. Folk musicians turn up in Mountain View for impromptu sessions on the courthouse lawn or anywhere the urge to play hits them.

Above: People say that Indians called Blue Spring near Owls Bend "Spring of the Summer Sky." The sixth largest of Missouri's springs with an average flow of 90 million gallons per day, it has been explored to a depth of 256 feet. *Right:* Lois Dodson quilts at the Ozark Folk Center. *Overleaf:* Johnson Shut-Ins are similar to the Great Falls of the Potomac, but are found in a more wild, rugged environment.